Heal. Grow. Love.

Cover Design: Pierre Jeanty & Patti Jefferson
Editor: Carla DuPont

For more information, please email customer@pierrealexjeanty.com

Heal.

Grow.

Love.

Jeanius
PUBLISHING

Claim your *free book* from Pierre TODAY!

Go to **wateringyoursoil.com** and
download your very own copy of *Watering Your
Soil* **absolutely free**!

The fortunate truth will always be that when a soul is in need of **heal**ing, it will always find itself at the feet of **grow**th, for it knows that without shedding, **love** cannot come in and hurt doesn't just walk itself out voluntarily.

HEALING.

The pain has held you for too long

You've been giving it too much room

to sit in your bones for far too long.

You've allowed it to dance in the depth of your

heart,

And hide behind your smile for too long.

The time to become free is now as it has always

been.

- Waiting is too close to death.

Today and yesterday shouldn't hold secrets to chat
about over your mind.
There's never good that comes from it,
they gossip about things that only yesterday should
know of,
things that will take today's eyes from its purpose.
Every day is meant to carry its own story.

- Yesterday's burden

Your mirror misses your smile,

That glow from your happiness.

That freedom you had in your skin.

The acceptance that swam in your eyes when you

looked at it.

Your mirror is calling your name,

Your real name.

Because it misses the real you.

The true you.

- Finding your way back

The journey of healing

is choosing to play the hands you've been dealt

while changing which table it is played on.

- Circumstances

And sometimes the only thing keeping us from

holding hands with our healing is us.

Not the weight of the betrayal,

Nor the burn from the pain,

Nor the aftermath of the hurt,

But our unwillingness to get up and choose

healing.

You've been an un-watered rose for too long.

Your thorns have been all that can be seen for too long.

It's time for your beauty to bloom again.

Not even for them, but for you.

- It's time.

Your smile deserves its smiles back,

Your confidence needs its confidence back,

Your love wants to love again.

Your peace wants to come back home.

Everything good that has left wants to come home,

you who knows the way must lead the way.

- Come back to the good

The secret to getting to a better **"you"**
is to keep shedding old skin and growing
comfortable into the new ones.
We often don't like change, but it's our only hope
to discover more and better.

Hardened hearts only become anchors that keep
beautiful souls from sailing.
Don't miss the beauty of sunrises and sunsets
because you almost drowned.

- Closed hearts don't get fed

Broken things can never come back to the way they were.

But broken hearts can heal.

They can become even better, stronger, wiser.

You're alive.

You're breathing.

You're here.

Are you living?

- Self Check

You are too much of a miracle to break.

Please excuse the thought that screams you are broken.

You did not break,

Your feet are tired from walking miles in the wrong direction.

Your ears had enough of failure's opinions.

Your eyes grew blind to your power,

You lost taste of the good.

All of you is scattered in too many directions, but you are not broken.

Pierre Alex Jeanty

You've forgiven their sins

and try to be their savior on too many occasions.

What would it take for you

to forgive you

without crucifying yourself first?

- *Good Friday*

These tears that are sliding down your skin,

trying to find their way to the floor,

these tears that are robbing your body of water,

these tears that you spill out because of your

feelings.

please do not let them fall in vain.

Please do not let them become just mourning.

Let them become a reminder that they could not

bring anything besides pain to the table.

Let them remind you how they came to taste the

best part of your heart with the intention never to

serve you theirs.

Let them be the lesson that teaches you how to

choose better.

Let them be the reason you never find your way

into their hold ever again.

Please do not waste those tears.

Please do not run back to the hands that could not

hold you.

Please shed the tears but let them be the reminder

that you should never beg for a heart that cannot

love you.

You are worthy of wings,

No one dressed in flesh has a halo at all times.

You are worthy of love.

You deserve good.

You are good.

The lessons,

they are light to a better path,

they are not billboards to remind you that you are

parked on the wrong side of life.

They aren't meant to be red lights for your life but

yellow ones.

- Cautions

Healing is when your smile

Doesn't hide anything

but shows what has been

hidden inside you.

Take your heart back from them.

They've taken enough already,

Don't let them continue to take what they

shouldn't have access to.

-Take your heart back from them.

You are the greener grass.

But you…

…let the drought suffocate it.

…kept sunlight from it.

…did not nourish it.

You are the greener grass.

You just forgot to keep it green.

- Water your soil.

The things you are regretful for

regret becoming one of your memories.

They hate being stuck in your present

and dragged to your future.

They want to go home and live happily in the past.

- Dwelling

You need you,

whether they want you or not.

You need to want you.

The healing is how you grow courage
to open your hand and trust that no prey
will snatch your innocent heart again.
It's how you allow your wings
to practice being one with gravity,
it's how you allow yourself to breathe.

I get it.

You miss what used to be,

but you also are missing the better that is coming.

Better, will never be choosing to leave

before the better you are looking for shows up.

I promise you that better will come,

but only if you stick around to welcome it.

Please don't ever think that leaving life is how you

welcome better.

Trust me,

I've been where you are.

Better will show up.

You are even on its Christmas list.

Please hold on.

- Choosing the end is never a better ending

You carry sunshine inside of you,

even your darkest days do not have the power to

make you surrender your brightness.

It is you who has to surrender it,

Feel the pain,

so you can give your feelings to the healing.

Call your toothbrush patience

Pour some grace on it.

Let both find your mouth

I promise you they will brush

every bit of bitterness off your tongue.

- Clean mouth

Those who left us don't have the right to build

homes in our minds

and invite all the what-ifs to dinner.

You gave them an inch

and now you're giving them a foot.

Find the time to take deep breaths.

These are the simple things in which we fail to see

their worth and beauty at times.

Your healing will come on your own time.

When you wait for it to come on its own,

it will keep missing the bus.

The hands of the clock will never call its number

Be responsible for your healing,

be proactive about keeping it when it comes as

well.

- Heal. Grow. Love.

The sun itself is waiting on your sunshine.

It is inspired by you.

You may not always believe this

but please always allow your light to be.

Apologies trapped in throats of the guilty shouldn't hold your innocence hostage.
It will attack your peace, but never give it the freedom to become your master.

- Be the one who apologizes to you.

Pierre Alex Jeanty

Your pillow deserves to drink tears of joy as well,
your ceiling is dying to stare into your happy eyes.
Your body will one day be home,
and your home will be soaked in laughter.

Eventually,

the scars sink into your skin,

The wounds become stories,

The pain cannot remember your name.

Eventually,

it all gets cast into the back of your mind.

- It's not meant to stay.

The forgiving,

it's the loudest voice to healing's ears.

It is milk for the thirsty heart and honey for the

bitter taste in its mouth.

The forgiving is what makes the healing taste so

sweet and gives strength to your aching bones.

Healing is diving into unknown waters,

It's being willing to plant seeds in places you are unsure it will grow,

It's learning to grow roots even when things are muddy,

It's letting your cry for help be heard and accepting helping hands.

It's answering to the voice of maturity before ego gets a word in.

It's losing in order to win.

Healing is often not what we plan and expect, it's always all that we need to accept and embrace.

- The boat doesn't tell the river where to go.

Acknowledging the power of the pain is the eviction notice to it. Healing is the authority that forces it to leave along with its belonging.

Pain is not something that just leaves, it's something that slithers its way to the deepest part of us, hides itself in the cracks of our soul and tries to conquer every part of our life. Despite what led it to find us, whether it is heartbreak, death, or loss of something, it's still a powerful drug that will impair your life. The solution to it must be healing. Healing has to be the go-to, it has to be the first option rather than the last resort. Healing's job is to sober you up to get the best from life.

As you chase healing, you must understand these things about it. 1.) It is not something that just happens, it's not a one-time event, it's a constant choosing to stay ahead of the pain and reminding yourself that your heart deserves better. It's fighting to stay consistent at fighting against the pain and the hurt. 2.) Healing is not a one size fit all. What I do for my healing might be totally different than what you do for yours. Depending on the pain, healing also carries different meanings. As you chase healing, you want to keep your eyes in the mirror, you must look deep within yourself, as well as being honest with yourself. How far you have to dig to get to where you need to be will be personal to you.

Lastly, know that you will never fully catch healing, we will always be healing from something. The reality is that what we are healing from changes, what it requires from us changes. You're always the boat, doing whatever you need to stay in the river and healing is the river, it will take you different places, with different sceneries, with different weather.

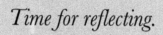

Time for reflecting.

Heal. Grow. Love.

What are you looking to heal from?

_____

_____

_____

_____

_____

_____

_____

_____

_____

_____

_____

_____

What have you been doing to invite healing?

_____

_____

_____

_____

_____

_____

_____

_____

_____

_____

_____

_____

_____

_____

Express how it all feels, clear all your thoughts here.

_____

_____

_____

_____

_____

_____

_____

_____

_____

_____

_____

_____

_____

Heal. Grow. Love.

GROWING.

Your pace is never slow,
It simply feels slow when your eyes are focused on
others' paces which ultimately make it hard to stay
in your lane.

- You're only running against you, against time, against life.

Grow, you caterpillar.

Wings will sprout out of those heavy shoulders.

Pruning your friends list isn't a childish act.
It's building courage not to let dead leaves keep
existing in space meant to give life to new ones.

- Detoxing

Let saying NO be part of your growth because it
will always be part of your love for yourself.
Loosen your lips and say no to the burdensome
favors, the meaningless sacrifice, the
uncomfortable questions and the questionable
things that aren't worth it.
Let saying NO become one of your biggest yes-es.

That torch you've been carrying to help others get
through their darkness,
you have to learn to pass it on.
You may never lose shade from lighting others'
candles, but you can eventually burn out.

- Dying flame

Pierre Alex Jeanty

When you outgrow people,

they will make you feel guilty for outgrowing them.

They'll try to make you responsible for their lack

instead of choosing to elevate higher.

The thing about life is that it goes on regardless of

who comes with you.

Eventually,

you stop trying to run from these things.

The heartbreak, the messy life, the fading

friendship, the list goes on.

You learn to prepare yourself when they come.

- Life

People do not evolve in easy.

They do not taste better where there is comfort.

Growing pains are how you get a leg up.

The journey to growth comes with its own pain.

-Uncomfortable truth

There's so much clarity that comes from living your truth, let your truth live.

Anger is a visitor that you cannot keep from
showing up,
but if it's staying too often,
you must do whatever it takes to burn down where
it's finding roots.

Doubts,

they come to block your path, but they are not

roadblocks.

They are merely speed bumps,

distractions,

rather than a force with the ability to stop you

from reaching your destination.

- Unstoppable

Everyone has opinions

but not everyone lives their own truth.

You are not everyone and their opinions don't

have to become your truth.

Your body is home.

Do some house cleaning.

Leave nothing clogged.

Do not let bones collect dust and become rusty.

The healthy route is paved by love.

- Care for your temple

Hold on to their memories.

Celebrate them in living your life more.

If they were here, they would want you to chase your dreams, they would want you to give fewer days to mourning.

They would want you to let go of what your hands cannot hold, change what you can.

Them no longer existing is a reminder that you must do more than exist.

- R.I.P.

Even after winter has come, let it all fall.

Don't carry it into new seasons.

Give room for new leaves, new branches.

Growth doesn't grab a megaphone and announce its presence.

It doesn't find fulfillment in making a decorated entrance.

It's only when growth isn't near that voices shout its name.

Growth will creep unaware and show up when it is needed.

It's like the water dripping on the rock.

Eventually it becomes where the rock used to be.

- I've grown, I'm not the same person.

The blooming is when you see yourself
with kind eyes,
carry a little more grace for your reflection,
and speak of forgiveness as if it's your last name.

- Say nice things about yourself.

To be filled with anything new,

The old has to be poured out.

Let it all fall from your eyes.

Don't be ashamed of your cleansing.

- Crying out loud

Time is on your side,

Look at the way oxygen flows through you.

Look at the way your eyes come undone every morning.

Days above ground are opportunities to grow new leaves.

- Being alive

Do not fear love.

Fear only knows how to keep you from love.

Even the black butterfly has wings.

Even the black cat has nine lives.

Even the black sheep is soft.

Even the stars need the black sky.

- Acceptance

Those who can command your peace

will always be your commander.

You only own your peace when there's no one to

take it from you and break it into pieces.

It's okay to be fire to those who've abused your softness.
Burning bridges that have made an open road for negativity in your life is a worthy sacrifice.

The smiles that knew your face before them will
show up once again even long after their ghost no
longer plays with your memory.
As long you don't stop trying to smile.

When you watch what you pour into your soul,

whether it be from your timeline,

your TV screen,

from the lips of those you know.

It becomes easier not to mix salt with sugar and

separate the sweetness from the things that make

your life sour.

- Detoxing #2

Perfect only looks good from far away,

Close up, you either see the imperfections or you

see the draining that comes with chasing it.

Your response to them choosing themselves should
always be you choosing you.
Choosing you is the perfect way to handle those
who cannot choose to love you.

In trying to prove people wrong, we sometimes
make them right.
The goal is to be right in the eyes of God and in
your mirror,
along with the eyes of your loved ones.
As for everyone else,
let them see what they want to see.
They'll choose to stay blind to any way that isn't
their way anyway.

Waste no breath on those who mistake your
passion for fragility.
How can they feel the power of sensitivity when
they only know how to be numb?

Speak with fewer words.

They'll spend more time learning what you mean.

Perhaps, that's how'll they'll learn to understand

when they finally try to.

- Give fools less.

These parts of yourself that you want to bury are
still part of you.
To get rid of them is not the answer,
how you make them bow to your voice is the
question.

You can't be light to the blind.
They will always see you as darkness
Stop trying to be good for them
Be good to you.

Honesty makes it easy for truth to take off its shoes
and relax on the couch to talk about the beautiful
things that matter.
Those who cannot appreciate it from your lips
don't care about what truly matters.

You and the future have a lot to talk about.

Just be present.

Let your tired eyes and your sore bones find rest.

It is how they'll grow strong again.

It is how you'll find new strength.

Resting isn't a sin.

The sun doesn't ask God's approval to shine.
It only does what it has been created to be.
Why do you need approval to be who you are
created to be?

Tomorrow never comes.

It only shows up today.

Why are you waiting for tomorrow when you have today?

Do it now, whatever it is.

Growth looks good on you!

Healing looks amazing on you.

Maturity looks sexy on you.

Love looks beautiful on you.

- Happiness looks happy on you.

Let the past be.

It has happened.

It has smelled the flowers

And encountered its death.

You can only live for what's to come, it has more

to celebrate and takes less energy than trying to

resurrect what can never become a miracle.

- Another reminder

When we grow is when everything with self finds each other. It finds confidence, care, awareness, love, acceptance, and even more.

- *True self comes from growth.*

You will realize you are enough when you

recognize there is no measuring stick.

It's all made up.

The ruler itself doesn't even know the rules.

Give yourself flowers.

The sooner you do for you what others can't,

the more you learn to be dependent on you.

- *Self-love*

There are those who will only bring flowers when you are dead and those who death won't be enough to convince them you deserve them.

- Again, give them to yourself.

Only those who do not know how to be soft will
call it a weakness.
How can you not misinterpret a language you
don't speak?

The fire will mold you but when it seems to be turning ashes more than giving life to new things, become the fire and do the molding.

- When what is meant to kill you is killing you.

You are a finished piece of art that you will have to
trace over as the bigger picture comes to life.
In other words,
you are God's finished work who will always be
becoming.

You've been wearing these experiences as long as
you can remember.
Life is always teaching,
let your heart come undone to meet the new ones.
I promise you love will have new experiences for
you.
You'll have to undress yourself of those old ones to
bathe in new ones.

Growth is sign that you are living, it is an even better sign that you are ready for love.

Growing is uncomfortable, it requires change, it asks of us to swim into new waters and step foot on new lands. It's not easy but it is the thing that makes our journey here better. It's the thing that opens us up to receive blessings we cannot receive when we are stuck in our old ways. Growing is part of loving ourselves.

Therefore, choose to grow, choose to evolve. Gladly let it pull you out of your comfort zone, gladly make those tough decisions. Complacency is an enemy and insanity is often described as repeating the same thing yet wanting different results. You are punishing yourself when you choose not to grow. You are meant to continue changing, even life rotates in seasons. Don't remain the same.

Heal. Grow. Love.

Time for reflecting.

What have you grown out of over the last year?

_____

_____

_____

_____

_____

_____

_____

_____

_____

_____

_____

_____

_____

_____

What stretched you the most?

_____

_____

_____

_____

_____

_____

_____

_____

_____

_____

_____

_____

How has it changed your life for the better?

_____

_____

_____

_____

_____

_____

_____

_____

_____

_____

_____

_____

_____

What are some things you are looking to grow from in the near future?

_____

_____

_____

_____

_____

_____

_____

_____

_____

_____

_____

_____

_____

Heal. Grow. Love.

LOVING.

Every missed opportunity to love is punishing the heart without cause.

Forfeiting who you are shouldn't be the ransom
you have to pay to the thief who stole your heart
with no intention of loving you right.

When love locks eyes with you,

Don't look away.

Enough people run away from things they desire.

Don't let fear run your good thing away.

- To those holding out

The curtain of the night sky easily pulls back for
the sun to rise every single night.
Let this be a reminder that when it's your time to
shine, nothing can or should be able to hold it
back except you.
Until then,
wait for your time with a patient heart.

-To those holding on

Love should never be the wind

How, you wonder?

It isn't supposed to come and go like the breeze,

acting as if it's something that will never be caught,

like a moment that is felt but chased into nowhere.

It was never meant to give you summer,

then eat away and punish your flesh when winter

comes.

It should not leave hearts numb,

and blood boiling all the time.

Love is not the magic trick that pulls you in with

the perfect illusion, even when you play your cards

right.

Love is the real thing.

It's the sea; it will let you dive deep into it,

and you will feel safe drowning in it.

It will give your heart endless sunrises,

and will warm into forever.

The end of it will always carry beauty,

it will always be full of the unknown to discover,

but it will never hurt you.

It will put salt in your wounds,

but only to wash away the bad you've endured.

Its wave will be consistent.

True love was never meant to be felt but not seen.

It's present, it's evident, it's consistent, and it's

undeniable to the eyes, the heart, and the ears.

Love is never the wind,

it is the sea.

- Love is never the wind

Love rarely finds those who are too busy chasing
it.
Their eyes are too busy and hearts, too lonely.
Neither does it keep its eyes on those who swear
they are prepared for it.
They are too distracted by their own definition of
it.
It's often known to find those who are healed
enough and those who want it but refuse to be a
fool for it while they patiently wait.

- Open the door, don't guard it, don't tell it who to welcome.
Just open it.

It is not the holier than thou who taste heaven on this earth but the wholly-er than thou who taste the heaven that love brings to this earth.

- *Eden*

The day is coming when you will smell like

fresh love.

genuine love.

graceful love.

self-love.

true love.

More than enough times

Answered prayers come when people never stop

praying.

Keep on waiting for your answers.

Keep on praying your prayers.

- Answered prayers

Cold hearts miss warmth.

Their fire is only smoke signals.

They may treat love like it's the plague but it's

their secret weakness.

-Love them anyway.

You will never hear love's whisper until you learn
to write its name on your mirror.
Our eyes tend to recognize only what they are
familiar with, what they have seen before.

Love doesn't always give us who we want,
but who we need and who needs us.

- Know what you're looking for

I cried when I saw love walking in a white dress
toward me with a lovely smile.
I am here to tell you that tears aren't always
coming from dark clouds.
Sometimes it's from seeing love shine brighter than
the eyes can withstand.

- My forever

Starving hearts don't get fed by crumbs,

You can only feed them

lasting,

understanding,

persevering love.

Anything else will only leave them with more

hunger.

Crowns fall.

They shift out of place.

Adjust yours and remind yourself who you are.

Love never leaves.

People take their half-love with them on their way

out of your life, but it never leaves on its own.

It doesn't know how to do that.

When you find love, it will not be returning to you.

It will only be presenting you someone who's

qualified enough to say they know love personally.

Their opinions about you not being enough will never be enough to stop you from accepting yourself without conditions.

- You have to be enough for you

The meaning of love should not be spelled out
with the letters of your old lovers' names.
They may have shown you the meaning of love in
some moments, but they are not what love
encompasses.

Love doesn't cost a thing,

It costs a few things.

Like a heart who knows they are worth it.

A soul who understands the value of

communication and knows commitment is the

only true currency.

Fall into hope,

Its soft hands,

Its merciful ways,

Its life-changing touch.

Fall into hope

It's holding so much good for your better days.

Self-love is an act of resilience.

It is a war against society.

It's learning to win silent battles.

It's understanding that self without love is a poison

nearly as destructive as love without knowing self.

- *Against the wave*

The sound of love's voice will be recognized by
your intuition, your heart will know.
When it is unsure and your intuition is unrested,
that's the warning.
Love is neither inconsistent nor does it show up
with different faces.

- Masks

There's no better time to stop granting access to those who take you for granted than now.

- Giving is never the problem, but how much of that is received in return.

Love was never the betrayal.

It was never the lies.

It was never the manipulation

The disappointment

The hurt

The pain

The forgiveness.

Love may have been there, but it didn't stay when

those things started to find their way in.

When you are courting love,

Those who do not have it to offer will be offended

when you refuse to settle for something that

doesn't look like it.

Better to have given love your all and received
nothing,
than to have kept yourself from loving enough and
missed something great.
At the end of it all,
knowing how much you can love even the wrong
person shows how much more you will have, to
bless the right one.

- Worth a shot

Pierre Alex Jeanty

There's no better way to proclaim your love for yourself than to forgive yourself.

The storm never washes love away,

If anything,

it helps everything that isn't love float to the

surface.

- Waves don't last

Be true to you but be honest with yourself.
One without the other is how many sink in their
lies while believing they are standing in their truth.

- *Quicksand*

There is a self-love that will come that doesn't
need a hashtag, to be professed where it can gather
likes in the shape of love.
There is a self-love that will only be reliant on self-
acceptance.
There is a self-love that isn't the popular kind but
the most life-changing kind.
How well you stay in the lane is truly seen when
there's no audience to boost you in the race.

- No applause

You're the type of fire meant to endure the storm

whenever it comes.

The rain can't take your spark.

The wind cannot steal your light.

The darkness can't take your love.

You should never audition for love with

desperation on your tongue.

That is returning to the poison that has abused

your heart.

You do so with scars from healed wounds.

Smiles on the faces of your heart.

Patience directing your feet.

You will know that you've found self-love
when you cease to hate things about yourself
just because.

Give the genuine '**you**' permission.

Allow the simple '**you**' to be.

You've been misunderstood because they never paid attention, not because you are too complex. They have birthed these confusions on their own, don't confuse yourself with them.

There are those who are waiting on someone who
will make them love themselves and there are
those who are telling those people that love must
be at their doorstep before anything.
Both are right, there's truth to both statements.
Love will find you someone who makes you
believe you don't serve it while telling yourself you
deserve nothing less.

Never forget that love is the remedy.

It's always the source.

It belongs at the root.

It will never stop giving birth to new leaves.

It's always good even when it's not all perfect.

It is everything good.

You are enough for love.

You are worthy of love.

You deserve love.

You need love.

You are loved.

- If you ever believe that love hasn't come because you are none of these things.

It is when we do not know what love looks like that we get swallowed by hate either from ourselves or from others.

Enough of us gladly accept an untrue version of love because we don't know what it looks like. We go by society's standard of what love should look like in our mirror when we are not meant to be like everyone and everyone else is not true to themselves. We also define love by what we are hungry for, whether it's our immature days when we craved attention and notoriety or in our more mature days seeking it in connection and authenticity. Not enough of us open our eyes to look for a love that speaks for itself; we like speaking for it, telling others why it is love or to convince ourselves it is true. We toy around far too much with incomplete love asking it to complete us.

The truth is, love is simple enough to be seen by the blind. It's not easy, neither should it be constantly hard. It's not meant to be chased our entire lives but to be lived when it comes. The secret is, love is a double-edged sword. It requires us to work on us while we wait on the love that is

coming from someone else. Unless we are patient,
we will settle for false versions of any love.
Love will come when it's time but don't let the love
you have leave.

Heal. Grow. Love.

Time for reflecting.

What does loving you look like to you?

_____

_____

_____

_____

_____

_____

_____

_____

_____

_____

_____

_____

_____

_____

_____

_____

_____

_____

_____

_____

_____

What part of yourself are you still learning to love?

_____

_____

_____

_____

_____

_____

_____

_____

_____

_____

_____

_____

_____

_____

_____

_____

What have you learned from your experience with the wrong love?

_____

_____

_____

_____

_____

_____

_____

_____

_____

_____

_____

_____

_____

_____

_____

_____

_____

List the beautiful things about yourself that are easy to love?

_____

_____

_____

_____

_____

_____

_____

_____

_____

_____

_____

_____

_____

_____

_____

_____

_____

_____

Heal. Grow. Love.

The end…

… Come back in 3 months

Write a poem about your healing journey.

_____

_____

_____

_____

_____

_____

_____

_____

_____

_____

_____

_____

_____

_____

_____

Write a poem here about your growth.

_____

_____

_____

_____

_____

_____

_____

_____

_____

_____

_____

_____

_____

_____

Write about about falling in love with yourself.

_____

_____

_____

_____

_____

_____

_____

_____

_____

_____

_____

_____

_____

_____

_____

_____

_____

_____

_____

_____

_____

_____

_____

_____

_____

_____

_____

_____

_____

_____

Other books by Pierre

Free Book

Watering Your Soil

Download at **wateringyoursoil.com**

Best-Sellers

HER

HER Vol. 2

HIM

Ashes of her Love

Unspoken Feelings of a Gentleman

To the Women I Once Loved

Sparking Her Own Flame

Other Books

Unspoken Feelings of a Gentleman II

In Love with You

Apologies That Never Came

Really Moving On

Coming soon

HER III

HEart

All available at pierrejeanty.com